Flight from Hell
in the
Heavens

Copyright © 2019 by Alicia Mo'Batti. All rights reserved.

No part of this publication may be reproduced, stored in a retrieval system, or transmitted in anyway by any means, electronic, mechanical, photocopy, recording or otherwise without the prior permission of the author except as provided by US copyright law.

Published By: PURPLE EYE PUBLISHING

Cover Design By: Pro_design37

Editing By: Sharman J. Monroe, ItsYourVoiceOnlyBetter.com

Formatted By: fiverr.com/farhaniqbal786

ISBN No.978-1-7331573-0-8

Dedication & acknowledgements

This book is dedicated to my grandchildren, Nico and Gianna. One day this generational curse of lies and dysfunction will be broken and we will be allowed to love each other, unconditionally, physically, mentally, emotionally and Tenderly. I hope my Memoirs will help you to understand, LOVE is the key. I love and miss you both so, so MUCH!

I would like to First acknowledge my Creator and Truth for the god in me that has arrived, Ase'.

I would like to thank and acknowledge Ms. T.Hicks for being the spark behind this new beginning, and your faithfulness as a steady and ride to die friend. You open this door and I am forever grateful. Peace, Love, Light and high vibrations to you and yours, I love you gurl.

I would also like to acknowledge my mother, Darlene Batti, MOM, you have been through hell and back. You are a strong woman and a mighty Beacon of light. I LOVE you to the Core.

HERCULES VERNON JOHNSON , thank you for giving me the Fatherly love and protection so desperately needed, I LOVE YOU!

Zoli Osaze, thank you for being there for me through thick and thin when nobody else was. I LOVE YOU!

Thank you Robert Watson, Michael Bolivar for your part in making this happen. I love you.

Thank you to my goddaughters, Nova, Simone, Katelyn and Juana for loving me UNCONDITIONALLY ! (you too Victoria) Love Y'ALL so much.

I acknowledge Ms. Betty Bell for her role in my life as a second mom, I LOVE you.

GodMother, Virginia Molden, your unconditional love for me is medicine for the soul, I LOVE You.

I truly thank and acknowledge the Cobbs family for your loving support. Much LOVE!

As for those who have been against me, I acknowledge and

THANK you so much for pushing me into my destiny, I love you too.

Table of Contents

CHAPTER 1: Work It Out 7

CHAPTER 2: DADDY, PLEASE DON'T! 21

CHAPTER 3: FORGIVENESS 30

CHAPTER 4: WHY, WHY, WHY! 42

CHAPTER 5: TRANSFORMATION 53

CHAPTER 6: Ole' On-Time Faithful Servant 60

CHAPTER 7: Flight from Hell 68

CHAPTER 8: Heaven Awaits 85

CHAPTER 1: Work It Out

My provider. My protector. He was my abuser. He was my molester. He is now my deceased father. I loved him with all his misery. He, however, never discovered the truth. The abuse was in every facet, physical, mental, verbal and yes, sexual. But at seven years of age I told my older sister, "He wouldn't do this to us if he was in his right mind." How the hell a seven-year-old could know that was revealed in time.

After a tedious day at work, I pulled into my new, two-car garage, and after gathering my belongings, I restlessly made my way into the newfound blessing acquired from my hard work, my new two-bedroom home. It wasn't long before the ringing of the telephone was screaming for my attention.

I let the answering machine relieve me from the task of talking to the caller. I was emotionally drained; I had no attention to give. I settled in, fed my face, relaxed and suddenly remembered the answering machine was waiting. I noticed the light blinking and only one message was in the cue. It was my cousin in the State of Washington with news of distress. With all the energy left in my index finger, I began to touch the numbers.

She answered with an empty soul and said, "They gave my dad three weeks to live. It's his liver, and I don't wanna go through this by myself. I need some help, would you please consider helping me?"

Without any plan or know-how, I guaranteed my assistance. I would extend myself and services often to family and friends so this was nothing new.

I thought about my older cousin, who once was very close to my father, being they are first cousins. I made my way back to work the next morning. My cousin, Jay, who was slowly dying was on my mind. I was thinking about the times I spent with him the last time I was in Washington, and salty tears began to flow from the corners of my eyes. I pulled into the parking lot. I felt a little wetness on my face, and a puddle sitting in my right shoulder blade. I pulled myself together;

dried my face, eyes, and shoulders so that I could put in the eight hours expected, but I was in despair. I tried to figure out how to make the eleven hour journey to Washington State to help nurture a relative to death. It came in waves — the ideas, the suggestions — then I caught wind of the latest buzz going around the office. There was a loan processor position available in

Washington State, I was currently an operator in the call center, this would be a step up.

So, could I do this? I thought *I could pull this off.* This job was usually an opportunity for advancement after one year of employment, but I had only been employed for nine months. But oh, what the hell! Step out on faith. Speak things into existence and let's do this. After all, this was what I did best, so I was gonna have a little talk with God and walk this out. Not long after inquiring, I heard my God loud and clear, when I say God will let you know if you ask, trust me, He will speak.

I got a call after applying for the position, and asked the

branch manager to consider hiring me when my year was turned in. But to my surprise, I got this very unexpected response.

My manager came to my desk with the biggest smile and asked me, "Did you apply for a Loan Processor position in Washington State?" Confused, puzzled and a little reluctant to admit to her that I was trying to move on, I admitted to the application.

After a few awkward seconds she sternly admitted, "Well, young lady, I am happy to inform you that the district manager from the Washington Branch called my manager and told him that the job is yours if you want it." It was a done deal. Tada! I was on my way to help my cousin nurture her father onto glory.

I had made arrangements with my mother to move into my house, and be the guardian for my child. My daughter was determined to finish high school with the friends she loved and didn't want to move to Washington State. I felt the need to find and inform my dad. I made my way into the neighborhood that I had grown up in as an attempt to find him. He was now a homeless man because of a drug addiction problem. I would always keep my dad in my prayers asking God to help me get him off of the streets. I always made it a point to stay in contact with my dad as best I could. I found him struggling to walk down the sidewalk, pushing his possessions in a grocery cart with all the strength he had.

As I rolled up on him I yelled, "Hey Dad!" He turned towards me and smiled.

It was crazy. In our conversation, I found that somehow, my dad was already informed about my new home and my leaving it with my mother to watch over my daughter. I detected that It seemed to make him a little jealous. Maybe it was my Aunt Mildred that informed him. I had confided in her when I purchased the house and discussed my plans in depth with her. I promised my dad that I would find a home, and move him in it as well. Dad and I agreed that I would correspond with him through his brother, my Uncle Ace. I gave Dad the biggest hug I could and kissed him on his cheek. We both turned away, and continued our journey to our separate destinations.

All I thought about was how was I going to pull this promise together. As I drove away, I had a vision of the civil engineer who once had it all, but I was watching this feeble old man struggle to push all of his belongings in that cart down the road. It was such a transition from the powerful monster who would beat me. Is this the same man who would beat me as if I was another man? Now, he couldn't knock my jaw off track if he wanted to. He disappeared in my rearview mirror, wobbling from side to side.

It was going to be a journey. I made arrangements to move to Washington State with an old friend I went to junior high school with. I'd just recently been in contact with him after several years of no communication. I packed my car as light as possible, said my goodbyes, and left my daughter in the care of my mother who graciously moved into my new home to take care of my baby.

After a disagreement between the old friend and I, who wanted sex that I was not willing to give, my original living arrangements in Washington fell apart. Overnight, literally, I had to find somewhere else to live. He woke me up at approximately 4:00 a.m. to let me know that if I didnt want to sleep in his bed that I needed to leave. I had to be at work at 8:00 a.m., so I gathered my things, showered, packed and slept in my car until time to get to work.

I connected with a coworker, who took notice to my somber demeanor that morning. We discussed my situation, and she generously opened up her home to me and we became roommates.

I worked in Seattle, Washington during the week and drove to Wapato, Washington for the weekends to assist my family with hospice care for my elderly cousin who had three weeks left to live according to his doctor. After three weeks of tender loving care, my cousin passed at 2:00 a.m. I had just finished a shift of caring for him and went to rest on the couch. Within minutes; I heard and felt a rush of wind run pass me, it would be my cousin, the daughter of cousin Jay, and another relative tapped me on the shoulder and asked me to come back into the room. It was finished. The coroner was soon called, after watching the coroner wrap a sheet around him, I packed up and said my goodbyes, and left.

As I drove out of the driveway I felt something bubbling up inside. There were those damn wet things rolling down my face again. Where they came from I didn't know. My strength was failing me. I was known for being strong, and not breaking down but I was breaking. That was an experience I will never forget. I watched cousin Jay go from driving me around to being bedridden and watching the last drop of bodily fluids drip from his nostrils as they rolled him over in that sheet. Three miles into heading towards home, I cried out to my Creator, "Lord, why? Why did you send me through this?"

I heard a very subtle voice say, "I am preparing you for your father's death."

WHY?

To my demise and my surprise, I lifted my

head in pain

I tried to drive, it took my sight and the wings of love steered in the rain

It's not my choice to take this plate and set it on

the side, just wanna know why? He is my father, I

love him and his beatings I took in stride

But now comes a time

and it is blowing my

mind Where do I look, to

go, where can I hide?

Okay so do I

have a choice,

do I have a

voice I do NOT

want my father

to die.

I didn't understand at the time why I had to be the one groomed for my Dad's departure, but I received the assignment given to me by God as I traveled down the lonely highway after nursing cousin Jay to death. I realized, with no remorse and with every ounce of gumption I had, I had to walk this thing out and see it all the way through. I would be the one to make sure my dad would rest in peace. He had no life insurance, and no money. All he had at this point in his life was me. I couldn't believe all I was about to face after all he put me through, but I would soon understand.

I was never bitter about the abuse. I was always puzzled as to why my dad was so mean. I was his favorite of all six of his children, I seemed to have gotten the most attention and beatings. I never understood his affection. My aunt Mildred and I were having a conversation about my departure to Washington State, one afternoon. Aunt Mildred felt the need to inform me of a comment my dad made to her recently. Aunt Mildred went on to inform me that in her conversing with my father about our next move, he informed her that he loved me more than his wife. I thought she may have misunderstood him so I dismissed the claims, but deep inside, I still wondered.

I imagined that this suffering of homlessness, mental disorder and dis-ease that was obviously fueling his anger was his punishment for the abuse and damage he perpetrated on others and was about to leave behind. Maybe he was suffering the consequences of his sins, I didn't know, but I was feeling torn. Whatever this was going to be, I was ready. I believed this would be a most important part of my healing.

As I glared into the dark, an old memory that would often arise began to prick my attention again.

I'll never forget. I got a phone call from my sister saying Dad had just left the house. He was looking for our mother, who was hiding out from him, because he had threatened to beat her, and take her check. Beating Mom, and taking her check was a regular thing for Dad, but obviously Mom finally had enough. My mom had made her way over to my old apartment that I surrendered to my younger sister two months prior. My little sister said she answered the door and told Dad that Mom wasn't there. She told me that our father said he would be back.

I was *always* the one they'd call when trouble arose. I hung up the phone, and made my way across town. The nerves were bubbling in my stomach, my heart was beating rapidly, my mouth was dry, and I could hear theme music in the atmosphere. The theme music from the movie, *Jaws*, was penetrating every fiber of my being. All kinds of crazy thoughts were swimming around in my head. The thought of another unpredictable encounter with my dad was debilitating, but I had to do whatever needed to be done to deal with him and protect my mom.

I got to the apartment in a short amount of time. I comforted my mom. My little sister and I put her on the bus, and directed her to our older sister's place for safety. We heard a knock at the front door within minutes after the bus pulled off. My little sister ran upstairs as I answered the door. I gently cracked the door open and greeted my dad, as he showed his face through the small opening. I could tell he was not expecting me and was confused to see me.

He asked, "Where's your mother?" I stated, "She's not here."

He stood in the opening with his head down and a small box under his right arm.

All of a sudden, he tucked his head and shoulders in and rammed the door forcing it open, and knocking me to the floor. He jumped right on top of me and began his ritual. He was on my chest, beating my face to a pulp. As I was screaming for help, I can hear my little sister's footsteps pounding down the stairway. As she ran up on us she was holding a crowbar and screaming at the top of her lungs, "Get off of her!"

I was yelling and screaming, "GET HIM OFF OF ME!"

My little sister smacked him on the back at least three times then looked down into my eyes while crying, "It's not phasing him! What do I do?"

Dad reached back and grabbed the crowbar from her then snatched it to beat me with it. But before he could get his balance, I growled, grunted and *pushed* with whatever strength I had. I did it. I pushed him off of me.

I flipped him over and Dad was now on the floor, and I was stomping him in the face with all 140 lbs. of me. I must've stomped him at least three times before I realized what I was doing.

I looked down and began screaming, "Why? Why do I still have to fight with you? NO!"

I backed up, and ran into a corner. There I was on the ground balled up in the corner rocking myself. By now, Dad was up. He grabbed his box from the ground, and made a beeline out of there.

My little sister ran to me, grabbed me into her arms and, in an attempt to console me, she begged and cried out, "Licia, please don't lose it! Please, don't lose your mind."

That would be the last time he ever put his hands on me.

CHAPTER 2: DADDY, PLEASE DON'T!

The loan processor job was perfect for keeping me busy and allowing my mind to breathe. Within two weeks or so, I was in regular contact with my dad, and traveling back and forth from Washington to California to be available and provide for my mother, and my daughter, and eventually be in attendance of my baby's graduation ceremony from high school. Milestones. I never really had time for myself. I was working two jobs, as a loan processor for, *The Money Store,* and as a mobile notary on the side to provide for two different households, and trying to figure out how to get my dad off of the streets.

At this time in his life, my dad was estranged from his family, most of his friends, and career as a civil engineer. He lost everything to drug addiction and was basically living on the streets of Sacramento, California. On this particular trip back to Sacramento, I was visiting with my younger sister. I was driving across town en route to drop my younger sister off at her apartment. In our fun and laughter of being in the moment and sharing stories of love and life, we saw a homeless guy riding a bike and pulling a grocery store basket with all his belongings right alongside himself.

We were amazed at how the guy was able to ride the bike, and hold onto the basket. We were in awe at how the homeless develop their skills to survive.

Then I asked her, "What if that's Dad?"

Suddenly, we took a second look, and to our surprise we noticed, and in synchronized harmony we both cried, "It is!" I think we both choked; it was not a good feeling.

I think I had hot flashes and mixed emotions all in one session.

My little sister asked, "Oh, shit, whatcha gonna do?"

In one swoop, I tried to get to him. I crossed the train tracks, manipulated a serious U-turn, and in a motion full of anxiety,

I whipped that car around, and pulled upon him. Needless to say, he was startled and a little discombobulated, as he looked in our direction. He had no clue who we were.

"Dad!" I yelled, "It's me, Alicia." His face morphed from confusion to a smile that lit up my heart. The sigh of relief for the both of us was warranted.

My sister was stuck in the car and in her emotions I, however, jumped out, ran to him and grabbed him in a hug. I fumbled around in my pockets for all the change I could muster, then opened his hands, and firmly laid it in his palms. I reminded Dad to look for my letters, via Uncle Ace, until I could return for him.

My little sister never got out of the car. I got back in and continued on my way taking my sister to her destination and I continued on to make my way back to Washington State. As I pressed on towards the freeway to begin my long ride home, I began contemplating a plan to get my dad off the streets. On this drive home back to the state of Washington, I praised and thanked my Creator for His guidance, miracles and direction. All the while, I was remembering the small voice I heard back in Washington State at 2:00 a.m. after the passing of my older cousin, Jay. The voice that informed me of my father's upcoming demise, and the role I'd play in his transition.

Why, oh why?

Back in Washington State, I engaged my roommate in conversation about my dilemma. She suggested we purchase a house together and bring my dad to Washington State. Even though I did not plan to stay in Washington, this sounded like a good idea. I just need to make things happen ASAP and it sounded like a plan.

I was supposed to only be in Washington State for six months regardless of my job change. I mean, I had just bought my first home in Sacramento, California, my daughter didn't want to leave her friends, and so I'd planned to just be in Washington State for the cause, and at the most, six months. This second house would just be an investment for future rental income after we remodeled it. Within two months, on June 11, 1998, I sent this letter to my uncle's house to give my father a heads-up on where things stood thus far.

Hey Dad,

Good news. My roommate and I found a house. The loan was approved, and we will be closing on the loan sometime around July 15. God is so good. You will like my roommate. She's nice. She is from Iran and she is Persian. We also work together.

There is a lot of work that needs to be done on the house, but I am gonna come and get you on the weekend of the 15th and take you straight to the house, to the mother-in-law quarters in the back. That back apartment is liveable and ready for tenancy. But I don't think my roommate and I will be moving into the main house for another week after I get you, so you can keep an eye on the house and take care of things for us until we move in.

We are not very far from the house, so I'll be able to come take care of and check on you every day until I get settled in the front house. I will feel better once you get here, and I hope you've been alright and are ready. I'll probably leave about 6 p.m. on Friday, July the 17th and arrive at about 6 a.m. on Saturday. I'll go to the house, get some sleep, and be on my way to pick you up at about 2 p.m. and we will get on the road so I can get back in time to rest on Sunday and back to work on Monday. We'll get a few groceries for you and take you to your new home.

By the way, my blood test came back negative. I don't have lupus, diabetes or thyroid problems. However, now they are going to do a CAT scan and look for mild stroke and swelling *on the brain. All my symptoms have been occurring only on my right side of my body — head pains, numbness and tingling in my hands and feet with serious hair loss and blurred vision. I'm thinking it is stress.*

I have been really worried about this house, my bills (two mortgages) YOU, my daughter, my dog who has breast cancer, and whatever else occurred in between,

Aunt Dora and Grandmother Daisy—but I am not trying to let things bother me. See you soon, Love, your daughter.

Sincerely and Truly, Alicia

P.S. Start the countdown

In the meanwhile, I had all this other drama going on. My ex-boyfriend Elliott and I shared a dog named Sade; she was our baby. We had to get our child, our dog, to the veterinarian to be examined. She had a large cyst-like lump growing on one of her breasts, which we noticed shortly after she birthed her second litter of sixteen pups.

After Sade was diagnosed with breast cancer, we decided to each go in half on the bill. We had just lost our other dog to breast cancer not long after her surgery, so we were keeping an eye on Sade, and were in constant prayer.

I had to make my way back to California. On this trip back to Sacramento, I decided that this would also be my only chance to steal away with my dog, and spend some quality time with her. Since I'd moved to Washington State to help my cousin with hospice care for her father, I had to leave Sade with my ex-boyfriend to handle the surgery. I noticed that after the surgery he was hesitant and didn't seem to want to take Sade back to my home in California, to my mom. I figured he was trying to keep her, so I concocted a devious plan to get her back.

My plan was to inform my ex that I was going to take Sade to the park for a visit while I was in town. That would be my opportunity, and then I'd make my great escape, so I did just that. Dad, Sade and I made our way back to our new life waiting for us in Washington. It was a pleasant drive home, as Dad read the billboards and signs along the highway. All the way, Sade hung her face out the rear window, enjoying the breeze.

We made a few stops to calm the hunger, use the restroom, and do a final gas-up so we could make it to the beautiful state of Washington. South Seattle, Washington. . . here we come.

CHAPTER 3: FORGIVENESS

There were a lot of things to adjust to in becoming a parent to my parent. Dad seemed to have his drug addiction under control, yet his dumpster diving habit seemed to be infused in his DNA. I tried to tell him a couple of times that he need not accumulate his treasures, and clutter up his space. I'd come in from work, and make my way to his quarters in the back to check on him. Dad would always offer me dinner, but I just could not indulge. His cooking habits were not inviting, nor were his choice of edibles healthy for the body. He would dumpster dive, and bring home discarded old food and eat it.

My daughter, Natalie, decided to come visit with me on her school break, as she was transitioning from high school to college. She was going through some teenage changes, but nonetheless I was ecstatic to have her in my space. Natalie never cared much for my dad, and I eventually had a taste of the insidious cancer that was festering in her on an explosive night of bonding.

On this night, we were all in the living room talking and attempting to get along. Dad was really trying to find an opening with Natalie. Even though she was trying to be cordial, she wasn't amused, and then he did it — my dad hit the wrong key when he brought up my mom. She exploded. Natalie let it out, and sliced him with that machete for a tongue that she honestly got from me.

Natalie broke my heart as she spoke of his abuse towards my mom, and I. She just seemed to have been cocked, and ready to fire. She was so exhausted when she laid her weapon down. I couldn't speak.

As Dad looked at me in despair, he cried, "Who has been feeding her these lies?

Is that why she hates me?"

I couldn't believe his denial, and yet my heart still ached for them both. All I could do was cry inside. A taste of hell, with no sign of the heavens. I separated them, consoled my child, and went back into my bedroom for some time well needed to process the event and some time to myself. But the visions of the past came flooding back to me.

It was after a brutal beating at the playground. It was after my curfew. I had lost track of time talking to a boy on the ramp. Dad came out of nowhere and I can see a silhouette of my little sis hurrying along beside him, my little brother was two steps ahead trying to give me a heads up, he yelled, "Licia, dad's coming." Before I could gather my senses, the guy who came to meet me ran off, dad walked upon me, slapped me upside my head, kicked me in the back, and told me to take my ass home. I ran headed towards the house like he told me to. As I approached the house I remember not being able to slow down to make the turn into our yard.

My body was in flight mode so I picked up speed and kept going. I ran right past the house. Suddenly I heard that familiar voice of my little sis,

"Licia, WAIT! Don't leave me!"

Then I heard a thud, I barely looked back and saw little sis on the ground reaching towards me but I turned back around and kept running. I ran till I couldn't run anymore. It was so dark, and every time I heard the sound of a car tire screeching, I thought it would be my dad looking for me so I would dive underneath a nearby parked car to hide. I walked until daybreak.

Finally, I reached my cousin La Rae's home and she took me in. But after about a week of hiding out, we heard through the grapevine that my father was going around threatening other relatives to force my appearance. The cousin who was harboring me decided we needed to call the police. The police arrived, questioned me, looked me over, then made the decision to transport me to the Children's Receiving Home across town.

I was processed into the shelter. I had to shower, shampoo and dress for bed. I remember looking at myself in the mirror. In glaring at that little girl in the mirror who thought she would never get out of that dungeon. I whispered to myself, "I made it out." I believed I was finally safe and sound, away from it all. But early the next morning, there was a voice over the loudspeaker. A female voice echoed over the intercom requesting for me to be sent up to the front office. After I made my way to the front office, I was immediately informed by a counselor without no explanation that my parents were on their way to pick me up.

I could not believe what I was hearing! I was devastated, I panicked as I flung my body to the ground. I began kicking and screaming begging not to go back to that dungeon. The officer who had picked me up from my cousin's house was standing there. He walked over, kneeled down to console me then picked me up, and pulled me to the side, holding me in his arms. The kind officer pulled me back from him, held my face up with my chin in his hand and explained to me that since I had no visible bruises, I had to return home. The officer then gave me his card, informing me to call him if my father had his way with me upon my return.

He then said, "Because I know he is going to do it again, and I promise I will come with cameras to take pictures."

Shortly after my mother arrived, we made our way out to the car. Dad didn't speak or look my way, I barely remembered the ride back. I was full of fear, and reluctance as we took the long ride home, back to the dungeon. I clung ever so tightly to that officer's business card the whole time wondering when it would happen. Dad had always told us that we had better not ever bring the white man — referring to the authorities— into his house. During that following long week of pure silence, I didn't know if and/or when he would address my running away and calling the police.

It was a Saturday night as I had just taken my shower to get ready for bed. I walked into the kitchen to converse with my older sister who was doing the dinner dishes before we all turned in. I was sitting at the kitchen table dressed in my pajamas. Dad was in the living room doing his usual chess playing, weed smoking and drinking with the boys. It was a trying week of not knowing. During that entire week, Dad would pass me in the halls with this crazed look of anger. I would flinch out of fear, and he would laugh.

Not long after I sat down at the kitchen table to converse with my older sister, we both took notice that Dad's company was wrapping up to leave for the night. We must have intuitively known what was about to take place because we both stared each other down. The door slammed. There it was — the familiar sound of heavy footsteps penetrating the house. The kitchen door slid open, as I heard the theme music from the movies, *Sasquatch* and *Jaws*.

Suddenly, "It," the monster, which is the nickname we gave my dad, made his way into the kitchen.

He mumbled, "I told you not to bring the mutha fuckin' white man into my HOUSE!"

Within seconds he was standing over me. He backhanded me in the face, and smacked me out of my chair. My body banged against the sliding glass door, and slid down onto the kitchen floor. Dad then snatched me by my hair so he could swing my body around to sit on my chest. Dad was smacking me in the face with the back of his hand, back and forth.

Eventually, the open-hand slaps turned into a fist. I heard a crack, as my scream now sounded muffled. My jaw was broken, and my cry for help was now a deep dark moan. I could not move. Dad placed his knees on top of my hands, as he continued punching me in the face, back and forth. In between the punches, I tried to catch a glance at my sister. I tried to beg her with my swollen eyes and muffled moans to help me. I watched her bury her face into her shirt as she tensed up standing over the sink with tears in her eyes and a dish in her hand. Suddenly, my little brother was standing in the doorway in amazement, mouth wide open.

After what seemed to be at least ten minutes or so, Dad rose up off of me, and paced the floor, cussing and threatening to break my jaw. After about sixty seconds of catching his breath, he started on his rant and tore into me again. Dad picked me up by my hair and slammed me into the sliding glass door. He then kicked me in my face, neck, shoulders and chest as I curled up into a ball.

For some reason, Dad took notice of the time from the clock

on the wall and yelled, "I'm going to get your mom from work. If I am this mad when I get back, I'm gonna kill yo ass!"

Dad made his way out the front door to pick Mom up from work. I crawled across the kitchen floor and when I reached the threshold, I made my way to my feet. I found myself walking down the hallway, staring out my brother's bedroom window.

There was that small voice behind me again, begging, "Please don't leave, sister." I needed not turn around to know it was my one and only little sister. I could barely see my little brother to my left with my peripheral vision. He was just watching; he didn't say a word. My older sister was standing in the doorway with tears in her eyes. I remember thinking *If I run out the front door, Dad may be hiding and waiting down the street. So* I climbed up onto the window sill, and made the jump down to the ground, then ran fast as I could. With my heart beating out of my chest, I ran down the side of the house, and around to the backyard, facing what seemed like a seven foot fence that separated me from the neighbors behind us.

It took all the strength I had to climb that fence. When I finally got to the top, I laid there exhausted for about ten seconds. I threw myself over the fence, down onto the ground. The moment I hit the ground I heard the neighbor's door open.

I heard a gasp with a shriek and crying, "OH MY GOD! I heard everything, you poor baby."

It was the woman of the house who ran to my rescue with her kids watching from the front porch. That angel picked me up and helped me through her living room. She sat me down at the kitchen table. She ran to the refrigerator, grabbed the ice tray, extracted ice, placed the ice in a towel and brought it to me to put on my swollen face. Somehow, someway, I had that business card of the officer in my hand, but I could not remember how it got there. I asked her to call the officer on the card, and she did as I requested.

Within ten to fifteen minutes, there was a knock at the door.

My neighbor answered the door and before she could say anything I was looking up at the same officer that made his promise to be there.

He yelled, "GET THIS OFF her FACE!"

He then snatched the ice pack from my hands, and threw it to the ground, and before I knew it, back to back light flashes from a camera, were blinding me. As things were winding down and I was seated in the police car, I could hear some loud noise of some type of metal objects crashing, and my mom was screaming for my dad to stop, as the officer swept me away in his black and white chariot. He took me on that familiar ride back to the children's receiving home, once again I had to shower, shampoo and stare in that mirror. I took notice to the broken jaw, the swollen face, scratches across my chest, and my fractured shoulder reflecting the *Hunchback of Notre Dame. ALL the while hoping this, would keep me from going back to the dungeon.* These are embedded memories that now play as movies in my mind.

The memory faded. I finally made my way to bed and fell asleep, hopefully to rest and face another day.

CHAPTER 4: WHY, WHY, WHY!

On a regular basis, I'd come in from a usual day of work, and make my way through the house, down the steps from the back porch to visit Dad before turning in. I would hear his music, and could guess that he was drunk and in his groove; drinking had become his new vice since quitting crack. I wouldn't visit for very long. As I entered, Dad swung his bottle in my direction and offered me a swig,

"No thanks, Dad."

I stepped closer to engage in conversation, and refused his usual offering of the food.

Dad must have worked up some nerve with his liquid courage, and he asked me the craziest question. I had just said goodnight, and was stepping towards the door,

Dad grabbed his forehead and cried, "Licia, why did you make me beat you when you was a child?"

With a gasp of air, I choked, and spat out, "What did you just say??" He repeated it again. I really do not remember exactly what I said to him after screaming at the top of my lungs, "WHAT THE FUCK? Are you fucking kidding ME?" I just remembered being overwhelmed with confusion, and emotion, and feeling like I was about to explode from the sudden emotional pain I was experiencing. That nasty old stuff from the past that kept taking over my psyche was rising from my gut into my throat. I knew l needed to release. I remembered running out the door, through the yard, up the steps to my backdoor, running around the living room, and throwing myself to the ground in my bedroom.

I screamed, "Oh God!, WHY? God, please help ME! I can't do this." I began my supplication. "Oh God, please take him off my hands. Lord, why am I going through this?" Suddenly I heard, "YOU asked for this burden. I had him all along. I didn't need your help. He was in My hands, carrying his cross, and you asked for it."

I heard God. I heard Him loud and clear. My Creator and I exchanged a few words, and I got the answers I needed.

Within a few months, I'd have Dad in his own apartment and wouldn't have to deal with him everyday. I had to make it quick because in the meantime, my roommate and I were having issues, and we decided to separate from our housing endeavors. I was falling behind on mortgage payments for both of my homes, and my roommate wanted out of the house buying partnership. We agreed to refinance the house in Washington so I could pay her back her portion of the down payment. So, being that I wouldn't be able to afford the house alone, while I was looking to relocate my dad, I also had to begin the journey of finding myself a place as well. In the meantime, life was getting back to normal as best as it could.

Dad could tell I was holding some feelings hostage. I had stopped going out to check on him, but he and Sade became pretty good friends. One Saturday a couple of days prior to my birthday, Dad came tapping on my doors and windows begging me for conversation. I let him in. He got on one knee to apologize and begged me to let him take me out to dinner for my birthday, so I granted his wish. Before I could dismiss myself to go about my business, as I turned away Dad grabbed my arm. As I turned to look back at him he said, "I love you, Licia."

I said, "I love you too." As I tried to pull my arm from him and continue on my way he grabbed me back again, looked me right in the eyes with this weird look and said, "No, Licia, I LOVE you." I blew him off in disgust and shrieked, "Ew, Dad no. Get out of here." I dismissed it knowing he wasn't in his right mind. I guess Aunt Mildred was right.

Things got back on track; forgiveness won overall. We both moved on after selling the house in Washington. As a bonding gesture I treated Dad to a Seattle Mariners baseball game before we moved into our separate dwellings. We painted a friend's house together as well. One evening I was resting in my room, and Dad was in the back in his quarters and my phone rang.

I heard my Dad say in a very stern voice,

"Sade is back here having seizures and foaming at the mouth.

I think you need to take her to the vet. She's not doing good."

I dropped the phone and ran through the house to the back. As I entered my father's doorway, I could see her shaking and foaming at the mouth. I ran to get my keys as dad loaded Sade in my car. I made my way back to the car and proceeded to the vet hospital.

The whole ride there I am praying, crying and looking back at her repeatedly begging her to hold on. When I arrived at the vet hospital, I jumped out, ran in and screamed, "Somebody please help me! My dog is having a seizure."

A male tech came running behind me, as I opened the hatch. He grabbed hold of Sade and ran into the hospital with her. It was nerve racking having to wait. Finally, about twenty minutes in, someone came out to me in the waiting room and asked if I would like to say goodbye.

I went in. I saw her lying on her side with her mouth strapped open, eyes closed, stiff and still from whatever they gave her to put her out. It was so hard and devastating to let go. I rubbed her, hugged her, kissed her on her soft fury forehead and rushed out of the room. I had her for eleven years and it would take me twenty years before I could even think about having another pet. First my cousin, now my dog, and they say it comes in threes. Now Dad's health started to prick my spirit.

Dad and I decided to watch the De la Hoya prize fight over a childhood friend's house. His name was Neal. It was Neal's house that Dad and I painted together. On our way to Neal's house to watch the De La Hoya prize fight, I asked Dad if he would let me take him to the doctor to get a physical checkup so I can get life insurance on him. I had noticed he always ate a well-rounded meal, and quite a bit at that, Dad had a healthy appetite, yet he was not gaining any weight. Quite often I caught myself thinking that these are all signs of cancer. He seemed to agree and disagree at the same time, not really giving me permission.

As kids, we had this name we'd call Dad in secret — Grin and Bear It. Since he was mean as a bear, evil and abusive, we thought we'd never get from under him, and we'd have to just deal with him, "grin and bear it." So, we did. But here I was, in the same position again, having to grin and bear it while trying to enjoy the fight because Neal had to keep asking Dad to quiet down during the fight.

In my mind, I decided that Dad had one more time to disrupt the enjoyment of watching the fight and I would announce that we would be removing ourselves so the others could enjoy the fight. Well, he did it again and I so very politely announced our departure. Dad's face was priceless when he heard me say we were leaving. I could see that the announcement of having to leave in the middle of the fight was frustrating to him. And I noticed the irritation began to settle in his chest. He evil-eyed me on the way out. Boy, if looks could kill!

I beat him to the car after saying my goodbyes. Dad slowly dragged his feet behind me smoking a cigarette. As he tried to enter the car with his cancer stick, I reminded him of his nasty deed he had in his hand and asked him to get rid of his cigarette. Dad threw his stick to the ground, and reluctantly adjusted himself for the ride. Two miles in, on I-5 South, he broke the silence with foul, toxic language and no remorse. Dad was calling me bitches, wildly waving arms around and cussing like a sailor while spewing his venom in frustration. I began ducking from his violent swinging gestures, trying my best to avoid another episode of a nervous breakdown that I could feel rising in my being.

Once again, a post-traumatic stress disorder (PTSD) episode occurred in my mind. I was back at the house on 45th street. My mind was racing, his mouth was moving, my ears were ringing, and I just wanted out. I remembered thinking that I needed to pull over, and throw him out, but then thought no — that 65-year-old man would never make it off this freeway. I knew I was definitely having an episode because I was ready, and willing to jump out of the car. So I did it — I snatched the wheel so hard the car flipped, but I didn't realize that until two months later in my recovery. One day as I was trying to gather my memory and recall the event and how everything happened, I could see it all very clear.

All of a sudden all I could see were tail lights in vertical position. I heard Dad hollering, and I screamed, "Oh God!" There was nothing but blackness until suddenly I awaken to Dad moaning. Everything had stopped, and a soft voice from my left side whispered, "Jesus loves you."

I turned to my left, and a white woman with white hair, and the sun beaming behind her continued to speak. She said, "He wants you to know He is here." I gasped and tried to open my door. She told me not to. I told this angel of a woman that I needed to get to my dad. Dad moaned again, and I pushed the car door open. I stepped out onto my left foot and, as I stepped onto my right foot, I went down, but I didn't feel any pain. I was on the ground staring into the face of the angel that spoke, as she was now holding me in her arms being the comforter.

How my car stopped and got to wherever it was on the highway I had no clue. How this woman got to me so fast was beyond me. As I lay on the ground looking up into her glowing countenance, I could hear sirens. Suddenly, I heard a man's voice coming from a shadow. He asked my name, but before I could speak, the lady placed her finger on my lips to hush me. She said my full name. The male voice asked my birthdate, and she gave him the date. I was looking at her with amazement. Another question arose about my age and she gave that info as well. I was amazed. I remembered trying to ask her how she knew this information, but before I could get any sound out, she hushed me again. Then she said, "I must leave you now." Before I knew it, I was out again only to be reawaken inside the back of the ambulance.

It was crazy. I knew my leg was injured. I had on shorts, and should've seen some evidence of injury, but the presence of this angel kept my focus on her. I mean, I never noticed any pain, never looked for blood or body damage. I was just in awe of this light. Before I knew it, I was in the emergency room with a curtain dividing my father and I. I had no clue he was next to me until I heard the nurse speaking to him. "Mr. Moore, I am going to remove the tube from your throat. Now, it will hurt a little so be prepared. You ready? Here we go."

As the nurse was instructing him, I could hear him grunt.

Then he projected the foulest venom of the day. "Where is that bitch-ass daughter of mine who tried to kill me?"

Before I could breathe my next breath, I saw the face of the nurse appear through the curtains with the most compassionate, yet apologetic expression. I couldn't help but choke. She rubbed my forehead and comforted me in silence. In my mind I'm crying, "Oh, God, *please* help me."

CHAPTER 5: TRANSFORMATION

The accident was on a Friday evening. I had doctors in my face telling me I would needed surgery on Monday morning. But by late Friday night when all tests were reviewed, things suddenly changed. I was told I would be going into emergency surgery in the morning. My right leg was crushed, and I was given the option of pulling a bone from my body, or from the bone bank to repair my crushed tibia and fibula. I chose to have a bone from a stranger in the bone bank instead of cutting my body twice: once to remove bone from another area of my body and once to insert that bone into my right leg. It seemed like the best thing to do at the time.

Later, I inquired about my dad and was told he was fine, and that he'd be released the following afternoon. Dad had had a mild stroke, so they wanted to monitor him through the night. Other than that, he was fine. After the nurse left, I tried to find the reason for his anger towards me only to be bombarded with another past childhood memory episode. It flashed through my mind, as the visions often did through no choice of my own — a symptom of my PTSD.

Dad was taking me by the hand and escorting me down the hallway into his bedroom for his routine massage. I can see a, eight year old girl's face, my face. I look so confused and bewildered. That little girl does not want to face what waits behind that door. Dad pulls me along through the entryway. He escorts me to the side of his bed, pulls his pants down past his waistline to expose his backside. Dad kneels towards the bed, lays down on his stomach, and tells me to climb on his back, and massage his buttocks.

Reluctantly I climb on top. As I am massaging him, I can feel him rotating his hips from side to side and suddenly, he reaches back to grab me and tells me to hold on as he rolls over. I am now straddling his privates. As Dad faces me, I am so uncomfortable. I don't know what to expect, but then it is obvious. Dad grabs me with both arms around my waist and leans forward as to kiss me. I am so confused, and that is all I can remember.

Meanwhile, I had a male relative named James, who had heard of my accident, and at the time, he was incarcerated but wanted to help. So James asked the mother of his child, whom I had never met and was living nearby in the city, to be available for me as I needed, and she so graciously agreed. She made her way to the hospital to be of assistance, and support. After surgery I was questioned, not knowing it was a screening, prior to being released. Afterwards, I was informed, that due to my responses to the questions, I would only be released to someone who could give me 24-hour care and my current living arrangements were not suitable for my condition as I lived upstairs on the second floor. So back to Sacramento, I went home to my mother and daughter.

While in the hospital, the doctors discovered a blood clot in my right leg. They gave me instructions on how to administer shots of Lovenox, a blood thinner. The blood clot was one of my recovery issues that needed to be addressed. I had blood thinner pills, Coumadin, as well that I needed to take in addition to the shots that needed to be administered. I thought my daughter and mother would administer the shots, but I was mistaken. I ended up administering my own shots.

My daughter was treating me as if I was a burden. She was very rude, disrespectful and short-tempered with no remorse she let me know she didn't have time for me and my recovery, as this will not be the last time she would tell me this. My mother split and left to venture out, and find her own space and rhythm in time. I was left crawling around on the floor due to limited use of my wounded leg. I was trying to keep the carpet clean, mop, and try to maintain my life, all while unable to work. I applied for disability and was denied. I was basically denied any and all assistance that would help me until I could get back on my feet.

I became a diseased soul, yet I was determined to walk this journey out. I went through some serious and rude awakenings in that house alone. I prayed, cried and begged God to save my home. My world was falling apart. My cell phone, gas, internet etc., were one by one slowly getting cut off. Eventually, I got behind on the mortgage and everything else. What could possibly be next?

One day, to my surprise the house phone rang. Could this be an answer to my prayers before the house phone, lights and my life got completely cut off from the outside world that didn't seem to care, or was this more drama?

"Hello?"

A familiar voice came through from the other side. "Dad?" I asked with surprise.

He answered, "Licia, I can't get anything out of your auto insurance. I need your home insurance information, and Licia, why did you try to kill me?" He yelled, "Licia, you know you tried to kill me."

Dad cussed me a little more, then stated he was trying to sue me, and he needed my insurance information. That cut me pretty deep, I was so confused and hurt so I cut him off with a dial tone. I thought, *it's just you and I God, just you and me against this ole' world. Please help me.*

My home was going into foreclosure, and I was finding out the true colors of lovers, family members, neighbors, and friends. Regardless of the circumstances, I was able to pull through with one miracle after another. One mellow day, I was laying on the floor meditating, and I heard my spirit tell me to get up, go out into the flower bed, and pull the weeds. I thought, *But I am losing this house. Why would I?* and I heard my spirit say, "Just be obedient." So I did. I hopped out into the garage on one leg, grabbed a hand hoe, hopped back around to the front of the house, and slid myself down onto the ground, positioning myself to weed the flowerbed.

I raised the hand tool in the air, tucked that shovel into the dirt, then turned the dirt over. As I grabbed the weeds to shake the dirt off I heard a soft subtle voice say, "This is what I am doing in your life. I am weeding out the bad, and whatever is left standing when I am done with you is what you move forward with."

In my emotional state I shed tears like never before. I weeded that flowerbed like never before. It was cleansing. It was a milestone, a shedding of weight to make it over this bridge from death to life. A bridge I would meet again.

CHAPTER 6: Ole' On-Time Faithful Servant

Some months sped by and I was healing, but I was losing my home to foreclosure. I was able to walk a little better, and was preparing to make things happen for myself to maximize my next move to a new beginning. As I packed a few things to be ready for the next move once the foreclosure of my home in California took place, I was standing in the kitchen window cleaning off the counter when, to my surprise, I saw my Uncle Ace pulling up. I said to myself, *this must be some crazy news because Uncle has never made his way to my place of residence.* Was it a pleasant surprise or bad news? It was either one or the other, no doubt. I made my way out the front door and greeted him along the walkway.

Uncle Ace was not smiling but he greeted me, and proceeded to inform me that my dad was coming to town and wanted to see me. A host of mixed emotions swept over me, and before I knew it, I lashed out at my uncle. I told him that under no circumstances would I see my dad because of the accusations from him about me trying to kill him. I didn't want to be tortured by his ideas and cussed out again. I just didn't want to hear it.

The buzz in the atmosphere was that Dad had come to town and left. I wasn't impressed, or depressed about it. However, as I was packing kitchen supplies on another day, once again I looked up only to see my uncle making his way up the walkway again. I thought to myself, *Must be important. Twice in one month is very unusual.* I greeted Uncle Ace at the door.

I stepped out onto the porch, and after the cordial formalities, he spoke. "I thought you should know that the reason your father wanted to see you was to tell you he is dying of lung cancer, and has only three months to live."

Okay, so now my chest was expanding, and those mixed emotions were back. Without processing the information, I lost it. My heart, my freaking heart, just sank. I choked, as I tried to yell with a dry lump in my throat. With every ounce of excruciating pain from the past left in me, I burst, and I let my uncle have it.

"Why? Why didn't you tell me the first time? You should've told me he was SICK! How fuckiing dare you! If you would've told me he was sick, I would've put my personal feelings aside. I mean come on! My dad is given three months to live and you don't tell me?"

Mixed emotions arose and settled in my soul. My stomach ached, and I was weak. I was hurt and so, so angry at my uncle, I stepped back into the house, and slammed the door.

After processing this news, I prayed and asked God to position me for this task. The phone ringing echoed in my soul. I asked myself whether or not this was my dad calling, I had a feeling and I now wanted to hear from him

"Hello?"

It was that familiar voice of my abuser. With a steadfast soul and a heavy heart I was ready to receive this phone call from my father. It took all I had in me to hold my pain. Dad's voice was so weak I almost didn't recognize him; the bear was gone, it grieved my heart. Once again I flashback to Washington after leaving my cousin's home at 2:00 a.m., and the message I received from God. I loved my dad regardless of the past. I knew he was a troubled and sick man, and as I stated earlier, as a child I had told my big sister, "If Dad was in his right mind, he wouldn't do the things he does."

My heart was breaking as he asked me to come, and get him out of the convalescent hospital in Washington. I assured Dad I would get there to get him as soon as I could. There was a lot of confusion about how Dad would get back to California from Washington. In my conversation with him, he made sure he made his request known that he only wanted me to come and get him. Everyone was pouring out excuses why they couldn't go. My grandmother, unbeknownst to me, was not in favor of giving me the money to go. Grandmother expressed this to me when she put funds up for my older sister to go as she later found out my sissy gave me the ticket instead.

Here was my dad. A man full of toxins, was now an obvious

threat in the convalescent hospital that was aiding him in Tacoma, Washington. Before I could get myself together for the trip, I received a phone call from the hospital. A very pleasant voice was concerned and inquiring if someone was coming to get my father. She also informed me that my dad must be removed from their facility ASAP! Dad was smoking while on an oxygen tank, and was out of control. The nurse said, and I quote, "He is going to blow us all up, so you'd better come get him or we will put him out on the street."

Honestly, I didn't think Dad would've cared if they threw him out. Dad was a diehard. He survived ten years on the streets after losing everything to crack. My dad had lost two homes, five out of six kids, his wife, a government job, and a host of friends and family, and most of all, his dignity. But he still had me, ole' on time faithful Alicia, as he would call me. The whole ten years Dad was on the streets, I would see him here and there, and interact with him. Heck, sometimes I would get the urge to go looking for him, and the determined, loving spirit in me, would lead me right to him in a vacant home, or under the freeway; it was nothing but God.

Arrangements were made, and I was finally ready, willing, and able to be the Earth Angel that I am, and make my way to Tacoma, Washington to bring Dad home.

The flight was nerve racking. I was trying to imagine how I would greet him, what he was going to look like, and how he was going to react to me. He sounded so hurt, and yet very humble in his request for my presence. After things settled between my grandmother and I, she mentioned to me that my dad may need to make amends with me before he passed. I had no clue why she was originally not in favor of me using the ticket she provided, or what her anger was about to say the least but it has passed.

During the flight, I contemplated this logic of hers until it sunk in. Oh my, this is my last goodbye. Oh, God, please help me.

Two weeks had passed since my promise to go and get my dad, I couldn't get his last phone call out of my mind. I could hear his faint, weak, distant voice crying out saying, "I thought you was coming to get me. I'm dying out here, Licia."

The flight was over before I knew it. I caught a shuttle to the convalescent hospital and made my way to the front desk. I introduced myself, and was asked to wait for his social worker to come and receive me. For the life of me I cannot remember her name, but she came with smiles and a firm handshake. She didn't waste any time informing me of my father's situation as she escorted me to his room.

As we were strolling down the hallway, the social worker felt the need to explain my father's foul language, and his ornery demeanor so that I wouldn't take them personally by stating that, more than likely, it was due to his illness. I returned her pleasant smile and stated, "Oh, that's just him. I'm used to it." We made it to his doorway, and as I was standing beside the entrance responding to the social worker, I heard a familiar faint voice say, "If it ain't ole' on-time, faithful Alicia."

The social worker left me as I made my way through the

doorway. I tried to present a smile as I approached his bed. Dad was laying on his side, skin and bones, covered with the thin beige woven blanket pulled up to his waist. This sight confirmed, and validated my anxiety for getting to him ASAP. Dad did his best to try and sit up as he beckoned for me to sit down in a chair next to him, and get comfortable.

He grabbed his forehead, and gave me an order, "Let me see your leg." I replied, "Naw, Dad, it's okay."

Dad tried to raise his voice as he again demanded, "I SAID, let me see your leg!"

In obedience, I slowly lifted my right leg revealing the seven-inch scar. Dad smacked his forehead as he focused on the scar saying, "I'm sorry, Licia. It was my fault."

Grandmother spoke it, and we both needed that very painful moment. Dad said that he was sorry. I couldn't believe it...FORGIVENESS. Painful as it was, Dad making amends filled me to the core.

CHAPTER 7: Flight from Hell

We had to get the bear ready for the flight, which eventually became our last fight together. The nurse entered the room to dress Dad for our departure. Dad rolled over, and curled up in the bed.

He pulled his sheet up, pushed the nurse's hands back, and said, "I've seen who I wanted to see. I'm not going anywhere." I tried to maintain myself since I could feel emotions trying to rise, and then, the floodgates burst open again.

I broke down, and began to cry. "Dad, I came out here to get you. You have to come with me so we can bury you at home."

I was now officially broken down, and didn't know what to do. Meanwhile, the social worker walked in on our conversation. As she took notice of the drama, she informed me that my Uncle Ace was on the phone.

She then walked me to the doorway and said, "I'll handle your dad. You go talk to your uncle on the phone at the front desk."

By the time I got back, things were obviously handled, as Dad had humbly surrendered his stubbornness. I began my earthly mission.

It was a struggle for Dad, every step of the way. Reluctantly, he allowed the nurse to dress him, a sight I will never forget. I watched him— he was basically deteriorating right before my very eyes. Dad was in agony through the whole process.

It didn't take long before we were struggling to get him out of the bed, into the wheelchair, and then from the wheelchair into their van. Dad moaned and groaned the whole time.

After getting adjusted, Dad was masked up with oxygen. He reached out his hand to me — a moment I will not *ever* forget. I took advantage of our first time of holding hands without it leading me into his bedroom. His first gesture of genuine, authentic love, finally. I willingly laid my hand in his, and to my surprise, he mustered up enough strength to give me a squeeze with a farewell look of despair in his eyes. He was saying goodbye. My heart was burning, I was full, watered down, and in my silent sighing, my heart cried out, "Oh, God, please, please, PLEASE help me."

Not a single word was spoken until we got settled in to wait for our flight. It was around 5:00 p.m. and our flight wouldn't arrive until 6:45. Dad told me he was thirsty, so I reluctantly went to get him some water. I was so paranoid about leaving him alone for just the short distance I had to go, but he needed to quench his thirst.

The airport was busy, and everyone was in their own world trying to get to their destinations. I was feeling so alone in this very large busy airport, as I returned with his water. Dad struggled to reach for and hold the bottle, so I assisted. As I watched Dad, I noticed he appeared to be hollow, empty, struggling and in pain, but trying to hang on. It was for me. He had said he was just waiting for me. He wanted to give up at the hospital in Tacoma, but he was holding on for me. My father was becoming my dad right before my eyes, right before he left this earth. The father I had always wanted was manifesting in his transition. It was only moments of loving, tender kindness, but I took it.

The announcement of our flight's arrival echoed in the atmosphere. Going back to California, back to Sacramento, to bury my dad. Who would've thought. As we made our way onto the plane, Dad continued to moan in such agony and despair as a flight attendant transferred him from the wheelchair to his seat. I sat on the inside window seat, Dad was buckled in the aisle seat. We got settled in. A flight attendant welcomed us with a very concerned look on her face. She asked if there was anything needed before take off and assured me she would be there for me every step of the way.

"Just buzz me when needed, okay," she replied, and parted as we patiently waited for takeoff.

I looked around the cabin. I could sense and feel a knowing coming from the other passengers; it was as if they knew my dad was transitioning. It was so quiet. I could detect the concern as well. Usually when I flew, the airplane was always full of chatter, baby whines, and a vibrant energy was in the atmosphere. Not this time. In recalling the look on the stewardess's face as she assured me she would be of assistance with anything she could, I was thinking, *This is gonna be one hell of a flight.* I never saw her again until the flight ended. During the entire two hour flight you could literally hear a pin drop.

Within a few minutes of our take off, I was at the edge of my seat with all eyes on Dad. I not once even thought of gazing out the window to take in the beauty of the heavens. Not long after takeoff Dad was pointing to the oxygen tank signaling to me to turn it up. *OMG! What the fuck do I do?* I was not given any instruction on the oxygen tank controls. I was sure the doctors knew this would happen, but I was not informed nor did I have a clue. I was in a position I did not want to be in, and Dad was in despair. I could see it all over his face. I reached down to turn the nozzle up, just a little. Within thirty to forty-five seconds, Dad was still asking for more. Now I was in internal turmoil. So I pretended to turn up the oxygen tank.

In my mind, I was thinking, *I am going to blow his lungs up. What the fuck! This is killing me!*

While trying to keep my panic at a minimum, I began to pray. I now knew the high altitude was not good. Then Dad was pointing towards his crotch. He mouthed, "wet" to me. Dad was losing his bowels. Tears were rolling down his face. Oh my God! In my mind, I was repeating, "I can't do this God. I can't. God. PLEASE, oh, God, please help *me*!" Then another moment of strength, confidence and faith kicked in and I took advantage of it.

Sitting right next to him I turned to my left, grabbed his hand, and told him, "Dad, there is nothing I can do right now, but we will land soon, and I gotchu."

God gave me strength...like never before. The rest of the ride was eerily quiet. Dad and I were patiently holding on. You could smell it, taste it and feel it —the stench of death was in the air.

Finally, we landed in Sacramento, and before I could look up and around, the plane was empty. A male flight attendant brought up an aisle wheelchair to transport Dad off the plane, but when I looked around, he had disappeared. I thought he was going to assist me. Here I was, standing in the isle, trying to figure out how I was going to move Dad from the seat to the wheelchair. I had no clue becuse when we boarded one of the flight attendants had transferred him from the wheelchair into the seat. I realized, once again, it's just me, so I bent down to grab his legs. But before I knew my it, my legs buckled; I felt weak. I sank to the plane floor and belted out a cry, "Somebody please *help me!*"

The tiny little stewardess who said she'd be there came running out of nowhere to the rescue. It took everything we had to lift him, and transfer his lifeless body of dead weight. By now, a totally different guy who I thought was a wheelchair escort approached me. He came to inform me that he was sent to convescate the oxygen tank because it belonged to the airline, and needed to stay with the airline. Instantly, my chest rose, and sank to my gut. I had no more fight left in me.

So with a faint heart and vocals, I cried out, "But he cannot live one second without it. He will be dead before we could get him to the front of the airport."

The escort looked me in the eyes and said, "I can't take the tank from him. I will just have to risk losing my job. Let's go. I'll escort you out front."

Deep down in my soul I was relieved and whispered within, "Thank you, Heavenly Father."

But the storm was not over yet. We made our way through the entire airport. It was about 9:30 p.m. or so, and the airport looked like a ghost town to the point that, as we waited out front, a tumbleweed literally rolled right past us, and on down the road. We patiently waited for the van, staring into the darkness. Dad soon grabbed my attention with his moans, so I refocused my eyes on Dad. His eyes began to roll back into his head. I leaned towards him, cupped his face in my hands and said, "I love you, Daddy."

Suddenly, Dad began to slowly raise his hand, pointing

towards the street. As he lifted his hand to point into the darkness, I leaned in pressing my face to his face, cheek to his cheek.

I ask him, "Dad, what do you see?" Dad replied, "Streets of GOLD..."

I gasped, swallowed and sighed. Dad's hand dropped back into his lap, as his chin sank into his chest. Then he suddenly lifted his head up, and leaned back. His eyes started to roll into the back of his head again. I grabbed his face again, and whispered into his ear, "I love you so much, Dad. Please hold on."

The van finally arrived after what seemed like hours, and the driver opened the side door, then dropped the lift to load the wheelchair with my father into the van. I noticed he did not seem to have any oxygen tanks in view, so I asked the driver about the oxygen tank. The driver informed me that there was no oxygen tanks, and that none had not been requested. It was my understanding that my aunt, and older sister had made arrangements for transportation with oxygen from the Sacramento International Airport to his destination at a convalescent home where a bed would be ready for him.

I screamed, "Really, are you kidding me? Are you serious? He can't survive one second without oxygen and the tank he has now belongs to the airline and they need to retrieve it. THIS IS CRAZY!"

The driver tried to convince me that we could load him up, and try to make it to the convalescent hospital anyway. I very sternly reiterated and let the driver know that was not going to happen. Now I was in a panic, not knowing what to do or where to turn. So I turned and ran back between those double doors into the airport to the payphone on the wall to call my older sister to find out what had happened. Boy, did I let her have it.

I exploded. "Where are you?"

My sister was confused and in shock as she stated, "We're here at the convalescent hospital waiting. Why? What happened?"

I yelled, "Why aren't you here with *me*? Why am I going through this all by myself? *He is dying!* And the driver is saying he has no oxygen because it was never *ordered!* What the fuck!"

My older sister replied back, and promised me that she was on her way. She put my aunt Mildred on the phone. My auntie began to explain, but I hung up, and proceeded to call 911 and requested an ambulance, I hung up and ran back out front to be by my father's side.

Dad and I were going back and forth, as he was going in and out, but trying to hang in there. I mean, Dad had just told me he saw the streets of gold. He was transitioning in the loading zone at the airport. I would call him back, but he would go back out. Finally, I heard sirens from a distance. My heart was racing. I was praying that we got Dad to the emergency room in time. The doctors had told us he had three months left. This could not be happening today. The wheelchair attendant was still with me, risking his job as we possessed the oxygen tank.

We rolled Dad back inside the airport due to the wind, and cold. I was sitting in a chair, and a still small voice spoke to me as I was watching Dad.

The voice said, "You've done your best, and all you could. Watch your sister's reaction when she arrives. Remember how she treated him in his last days he tried to spend with her? Take note of her remorse, her sorrow, and despair."

I believed my older sister would live to regret how she treated Dad. I mean, the last time she saw him was when she refused to open the door for him on Father's Day in 1997. We had been visiting with him a week before at her house, and she told him to come by for Father's Day dinner so it broke my heart to see him walk away after knocking for a good minute. I watched my dad disappear into the heat. I just couldn't believe she could do that, and live with herself, but she did.

I looked up, and saw her Cadillac pulling in. By now, the ambulance attendants were putting Dad on the stretcher. I watched her park, fly out of her car, run into the airport, and leap onto the gurney with Dad. Sissy was crying, rocking, holding Dad's face, and telling him she loved him, but I really didn't think Dad was there. I believed she was too late to express her love. Why was she saying this now when he could not consciously receive it? It was obvious he was transitioning and walking the streets of gold. It was too late.

For me, it was a milestone of a lesson learned with a well-deserved, and much needed healing session for the soul. I got to say my goodbyes. I was able to be there for him for the last time. For all the beatings, heartache and pain, I gave Dad love all the time. I, finally, in the end, found a way to recycle hate into love so that it wouldn't destroy my soul.

I've learned that loving unconditionally is universally required. Tomorrow is not promised. We have no idea when someone's time is up. Pick your battles wisely and decide what consequences you are able to live with given how you treat people.

Consciousness is required in this life.

As a child, and even as an adult, I always looked and longed and waited for love from Dad. Finally. Patience is a virtue. Love endures all. It took a flight from hell, floating through the heavens to get what I'd been fighting and pressing for, but it was worth it. That journey, that flight, was growth for me. It was a remarkably rude awakening for me. I had no bitterness. I held no soul hostage for my past. I am humbled, and forever changed from this life lesson. Dad is embedded in my soul, in my DNA. I am a part of him. He is me. We are one. Treat people with loving kindness, not just because you never know what lies ahead, but because you should treat people how YOU want to be treated.

It was one hell of a ride to the emergency room at UC Davis Medical Center. As

I was praying all the way, I could hear the EMT working on my father in the back of the ambulance. He relayed to us in the front the condition of my father. He was going back and forth delivering to me the painstaking symptoms.

He stated, "Uh, oh, he is leaving us." As he called my dad's name, he'd state, "He is back."

This went on for the duration of the twenty minute ride, which felt like hours. I was in agony.

Alicia Mo'Batti

By the Way

Hey you, you look nice today

How are you, fairly meddling, you say?

It's a beautiful day, ya

ought to cherish it in that

way Hey you, you sure

have a beautiful smile

You should

wear it more

throughout the

day There are so

many things you

can do

To show you care,

with gestures that

are true Bake a cake,

sing a song or simply

say I love you

It's such a special thing to do,

giving attention, spending time

With the people who are attached

to you, it's so easy to say

Hey, by the way, I want to spend a

moment, maybe find something to do If

you have just an inkling of a second, and

no allotted time to spend

So you say, you can at least take some

time to call or text just to say Hey, by the

way, I LOVE YOU!

CHAPTER 8: Heaven Awaits

Family members had been alerted, and the hospital began to fill with relatives. I never left his side during the duration of Dad's transition in the emergency room. I was pretty much the only one who stayed by his side. The others chose to stay in the waiting room. I stayed, and comforted Dad as best I could for the last time. I tried to talk to him to see if he was still present, but he seemed to be focused and starring in the opposite direction.

Dad's moaning and groaning began to get more intense as he glared at the ceiling facing the east upper corner of the room. I thought, *He must be in pain.* A male nurse stepped in to check on him. I asked if he could give my father something for his pain. The nurse agreed. This would be another last attempt to try and comfort Dad, to help him get his mind off of the pain.

I asked him, "Dad, ya wanna go fishing?"

He didn't answer. His eyes are now watering, and focused. But was it the pain he was tearing up about, or was he seeing his life story? Was he seeing the beatings, molestations, and cruelty he dispersed to his family regularly? I had heard, and was taught as a Christian that God shows us our life history as part of the transition from life

to death. Was Dad viewing a movie of his life? Were these tears of remorse for all he had done, and the damage he had caused and was leaving behind?

Dad had his eyes firmly fixed towards the heavens. It was as if the building we were in was not there. The tears began to roll into his ears, and the moaning became more intense. I could sense some energy approaching so I looked to my left, and took notice of my cousin, Dad's favorite nephew, and my older sister making their way into the room. As my older sister approached me she informed me that the doctor wanted to talk to us. I left my cousin in the room with Dad. We grabbed our brother out of the waiting room, and proceeded to a quiet spot in the halls to discuss whether or not to resuscitate.

The decision was made. We decided we would not resuscitate, and we wished to bury, not cremate him. I went back into the room. The others had already left and made their way back into the waiting room. Dad was still moaning, and it began to penetrate every fiber of my being. I just couldn't take it anymore. He was obviously suffering, and it was eating me to the core.

Before I knew it, I flung the curtain open, thrust myself into the middle of the emergency room, and yelled, "Somebody give him something for the pain! Please! Give him something!!"

The same male nurse I spoke with earlier ran towards me, slipped pass and dipped into the room behind me. I followed him in and, immediately after the shot was given, Dad sighed with relief. He took his last breath. Leaving a look of contentment on his face, the soul left the building.

I could see with my peripheral vision that people were coming back into the room. My cousin was walking up along side the window, and some others were following behind. I kissed Dad on his cheek, pressed passed the crowd, and left the building. I noticed my ride waiting in the parking lot. I climbed in and within seconds of closing the door, it happened again, I broke, I broke my alabaster jar, and poured out all the oil I had left in me. He grabbed me, and held me until I was ready to move on.

The flight from hell taught me to love without conditions. Dad did what he came to do, and he did it well. He came to teach me a lesson, a lesson well learned. Thanks, Dad. How are you going to treat your loved ones who are difficult or dysfunctional?

They are, well, we *all* are, damaged souls in need of healing. Every single one of us are worthy of tender love, a healing gesture or a loving touch. Look in the mirror and ask yourself: can I give what I would like to receive if I were them?

Who are you to judge?

Alicia Mo'Batti

www.ingramcontent.com/pod-product-compliance
Lightning Source LLC
LaVergne TN
LVHW091316080426
835510LV00007B/513